Andrei Ifrose

BURY ALL INDIVIDUALISM

AF470732

Andrei Ifrose

BURY ALL INDIVIDUALISM

By the same author:

Crucify all ambition
Glory in Sacrifice

ASHBURNHAM INSIGHTS:
  Baptism in Holy Spirit
  Blessing and Cursing
  Counselling
  Deliverance
  Healing
  Intercession
  Prophecy
  Tongues and Explanations

Bury All Individualism

TIMOTHY PAIN

KINGSWAY PUBLICATIONS

EASTBOURNE

Copyright © Ashburnham Christian Trust 1989

First published 1989

All rights reserved.
No part of this publication may be reproduced or
transmitted in any form or by any means, electronic
or mechanical, including photocopy, recording, or any
information storage and retrieval system, without
permission in writing from the publisher.

Biblical quotations are from the
Jerusalem Bible copyright © Darton, Longman and Todd Ltd
and Doubleday & Co Inc 1966, 1967, 1968

Front cover photo: Tony Stone Photolibrary—London

British Library Cataloguing in Publication Data

Pain, Timothy
Bury all individualism.
1. Bible—Expositions
I. Title II. Series
220.6

ISBN 0–86065–708–6

Production and printing in Great Britain for
KINGSWAY PUBLICATIONS LTD
Lottbridge Drove, Eastbourne, E Sussex BN23 6NT by
Nuprint Ltd, Harpenden, Herts AL5 4SE

This trilogy was inspired by three of the many Christian leaders who have moulded my life. Two of their lives made me start asking the serious questions which lie behind these books. The life of the third man pointed me towards the answer.

This trilogy is dedicated to that man, the Rt Revd Peter Ball, who personifies the principles set out in these three books more than any other man I know.

Contents

The death of Self

Lord, when the sense of Thy sweet grace
Sends up my soul to seek Thy face,
Thy blessed eyes breed such desire,
I die in Love's delicious fire.
   O Love, I am thy sacrifice;
Be still triumphant, blessed eyes;
Still shine on me, fair suns, that I
Still may behold, though still I die.

Though still I die, I live again;
Still longing so to be still slain;
So gainful is such loss of breath;
I die even in desire of death.
   Still live in me this loving strife
Of living death and dying life;
For while Thou sweetly slayest me
Dead to myself, I live in Thee.

A Song of Divine Love
Richard Crashaw

Introduction

When I began writing this trilogy I thought that the material would form volumes nine to twelve in the developing *Ashburnham Insights* series. I set out to write four short books on vision, community, worship, and service, intending to suggest in them that God wants to move us on from personal to corporate renewal, and that we should join Paul in asking to share in the sufferings of Christ as well as in the power of his resurrection. But somewhere between conception and parturition God, and an editor, intervened.

The first eight volumes in the *Ashburnham Insights* series were my attempt at a serious re-reading of Scripture on topics which, currently, are immensely popular. But as I began preparing this new material I realised that I was now focusing on subjects which people prefer to ignore.

When the material for volumes one to eight in the *Ashburnham Insights* was tested in public it received an enthusiastic welcome: some folk may have struggled with small details, but most people endorsed the general principles. However, I am afraid that this new material has gone down everywhere like the proverbial lead balloon.

One summer's evening in 1987, after a particularly violent and antagonistic reception at a Shropshire Bible

Week, I decided that enough was enough. I could not face any more vituperation and decided to ditch the material. But a few quiet words of encouragement and endorsement on the following day from the Rev Frank Cooke gave me the determination to press on and begin pounding my word-processor. So blame Frank if you find this trilogy unpalatable!

I prepared some rough manuscripts, sent them to my editor, and then flew to South Africa where I spent a month living with black clergymen, teaching them, visiting their congregations, and tasting apartheid at first-hand. It was a deeply challenging experience. After South Africa I spent some time in Northern Ireland. And it was there, gazing at the poppy-clad memorial to *Our Glorious Dead* in bomb-scarred Enniskillen, that I began to perceive the common theme which ran through my rough manuscripts.

I arrived home from Ireland to find an encouraging letter from my editor. He stated that some people would be so unhappy with what I had written, and find it so unwelcome, that he didn't know what to do with the manuscripts. After prayer, thought, reflection and discussion we finally agreed not to include this material in the *Ashburnham Insights*, but to develop it into the format of this trilogy.

I belong to that part of the church which is unashamedly both evangelical and charismatic. But in South Africa I was appalled to discover that apartheid appears to have as strong a grip on the lives of evangelical charismatics as it does on members of the armed forces. Certainly that is the view of most of the black Baptist clergymen with whom I stayed in the Transvaal townships.

It would have been easy for me to return home and denounce the white-led charismatic mega-churches of Johannesburg. But I suspected that if I had grown up there I would probably have been part of them, for they emphasised many of the things I hold most dear. They were not bad, but blind. They had a splinter called apartheid in both eyes. And I realised that if I was to take Matthew 7:5 seriously I needed to identify and remove the plank in my own eye before I could do anything about their splinter. That is what I have tried to do in this trilogy.

Books One and Two are my prayerful attempts at identifying the two critical planks which I believe seriously distort my vision and the vision of many other evangelical and charismatic leaders and congregations today. Book Three is my prescription for a course of treatment which might improve our vision, and so set us free to remove our brothers' splinters.

Whereas the *Ashburnham Insights* were written primarily for house-group leaders as hand-books for house-group study, *The death of Self* has been written especially for ministers, and I have primarily had a congregational application in mind. Of course I hope that these three books will also be widely used as a stimulating basis for a series of house-group meetings, but I particularly urge all in 'full-time Christian service' to work slowly through the trilogy, allowing the scorching light of Scripture to penetrate their presuppositions and experiences.

I am not a theologian. I am not even the full-time minister of a particular congregation. I'm just a man who has looked in his mirror and asked God to show him his planks. I have not attempted to construct watertight arguments to convince the staunchest doubter. Instead I've tried to pose questions which need careful thought; to propose omissions in our teaching; to point out imbalances in our emphases; and to plead that holy self-effacement and humble sacrifice may predominate in our personal, congregational and denominational lives.

I am sure that I must have got many things wrong. Even Paul admitted that his knowledge was imperfect. My problem is that I don't know what I'm wrong about; I doubt if I am the only person with this particular problem. Whilst I acknowledge it is unlikely that anybody will agree with everything in this trilogy, I do hope that everybody may be provoked and challenged by some part of each book.

Please read the books in the suggested order, and take care to look up all the Scripture references as you proceed through the text. Unless otherwise indicated, my biblical quotations are taken from the Jerusalem Bible.

My thanks go to all the members of both the Ashburnham Stable Family and the Ashburnham Parish Church for their unfailing patience, love and support. The following deserve special mention either for a contribution or for their company in a particularly formative experience: Ken Barham, Brian and Susan Betts, John and Marlis Bickersteth, Jean Breach, Teresa Clifton, Winifred Cox, David and Christine Freeland, Edmund Heddle, John Herbert, Sue Lindsay, Jo and Susie Marriott, Richard Martin, Margery May, Ralph May, Chris Nicholls, Jennifer Oldroyd, Alison Pain, David and Edna Parr, Catherine Rendall, and Roger and Penny Wilcock.

Timothy Pain

Bury All Individualism

O God of earth and altar,
   Bow down and hear our cry,
Our earthly rulers falter,
   Our people drift and die;
The walls of gold entomb us,
   The swords of scorn divide,
Take not thy thunder from us,
   But take away our pride.

From all that terror teaches,
   From lies of tongue and pen,
From all the easy speeches,
   That comfort cruel men,
From sale and profanation
   Of honour and the sword,
From sleep and from damnation,
   Deliver us, good Lord!

Tie in a living tether
   The prince and priest and thrall,
Bind all our lives together,
   Smite us and save us all;
In ire and exaltation
   Aflame with faith, and free,
Lift up a living nation,
   A single sword to thee.

O God of earth and altar
G. K. Chesterton

The
Problem of
Unity

I will have no fewer brothers and sisters than God has sons and daughters.

David Du Plessis

Few topics arouse as much apathy as unity. The proliferating annual conferences on evangelism are invariably well-supported. Seminars on signs and wonders draw vast crowds. Meetings protesting about abortion, homosexuality and Sunday trading are packed out. Crowded charismatic celebrations abound. But any event designed to pray for, foster and improve local inter-denominational relationships is doomed to failure. Very few Christians are passionate about unity. Most couldn't care less.

During the last five years at Ashburnham Place we have regularly arranged a weekend seminar on unity: it has never taken place. Why? Because not enough people have ever wanted to attend. Yet people have had to be turned away from our seminars on counselling, intercession, healing, deliverance, tongues, prophecy and praise. Only last week our local charismatic ministers' group voted against studying the topic together. They considered that other matters were more important.

Unity on a wider basis than their own immediate congregation is irrelevant to most men and women who, Sunday by Sunday, sit on the evangelical pews and charismatic chairs of England. They are far too busy with their own family and congregational affairs to waste time getting to know and love those who live nearby, but worship in different traditions. After all, the person on a pew rarely knows everybody in his own congregation; so until he is thoroughly acquainted with all these (even though some live many miles away), he cannot see the point of meeting with those from other congregations (even when they live in the same street, use the same shops, and have the same neighbours). And the man on a chair is not sure what would happen if his elder heard that he was becoming very friendly with somebody from another congregation—or perhaps he is sure, and that is why he keeps himself to his own tradition!

The men and women on our pews and plastic chairs are suspicious either of those who wear robes, or of those who do not; of those who use a service book, or of those who seem to make it up as they go along; of those who chant, or of those who sing in tongues; of those women who are keen to preach, or of those who place a hanky on their head before they pray; of those people who revere Mary, or of those who revere the Bible; of those who genuflect, or of those who dance and raise their hands; of those who believe this, and of those who believe that; of those who go there, and of those who won't come here. To these men and women nobody else is a *proper* Christian. They can't be. Because if they were they would undoubtedly be part of their congregation.

Unity on a wider basis than their own congregation is a nuisance to the men in our evangelical pulpits and on our charismatic platforms. They have to bury the dead, visit the sick, encourage the depressed, marry the foolish, prepare sermons, and ensure that nobody in the congregation is ignored or offended. They have not got the time for unity; and anyway they dislike ecumenism, abhor committees and mistrust the local Council of Churches. They believe that some real Christians must attend the other churches in their locality, but they can't work out why. They know that they ought to meet with the other ministers in their area, but they feel bored when they do and guilty when they do not. They half hope that somebody will die so that they will have a funeral to conduct on the day of the next fraternal.

These men are puzzled about how an intelligent man can either baptise a baby, or give communion to the unconfirmed; allow a yoga class to use his premises, or be so naive in his approach to Scripture; pray for the dead, or believe in the Devil. They divide into those who think that they defend the truth by correcting the theological errors of others, and those who think that they show love by remaining silent. In theory, they are convinced by the value of unity, but in practice they are sceptical about whether warmer local relations will increase the size of their own congregations. They appease their conscience by mixing with a few ministers whom they agree with and who are from their own tradition and denomination. If they meet another local clergyman in the street they are mildly embarrassed, but sufficiently professional to manage to exchange the necessary polite pleasantries. They cannot honestly say that they love the other local ministers; neither do they think that the others love them much.

Yet unity on the widest possible basis is vitally important to the men and women on the streets of England. The lack of unity between local congregations is their most frequently voiced reason for rejecting the Christian faith. They understand the different local churches to be direct competitors for their attendance, in the same way as Tesco, Safeway, Sainsbury's and Gateway vie for their custom. They find it puzzling when somebody drives past one congregation to attend a different one further away, but then they all know people who idiosyncratically drive five miles to shop at Tesco just because they do not like Safeway. However, it is beyond their comprehension when somebody refuses to use the local ecclesiastical equivalent of Sainsbury's, yet drives ten miles to worship at another branch of the same firm in the next town!

The archetypal man on the street thinks that all Christians believe they are ultimately on the same side (like a trade association) and therefore he cannot work out why they do not co-operate. He is amused when he gets six different leaflets inviting him to six different sets of harvest festivals, all on the same Sunday. He believes that the Anglican Church is the proper one, and that all the others are either slightly suspect or mildly inferior. He tends to be both simplistic and tolerant, not minding much what the church members do or believe, as long as he is made welcome, without being made conspicuous. He hates hypocrisy, and the disagreement, criticism and apparent lack of loving unity between Christians seems to him to be the most blatant form of hypocrisy by those who are continually pressing people to love each other in a practical way.

And to the Man in heaven unity, at every level, is an obsession. His ascended never-ceasing activity is intercession; and in John 17:20–26, his only recorded prayer for contemporary Christians, he urges, 'May they all be one. Father, may they be one in us, as you are in me and I am in you, so that the world may believe it was you who sent me. I have given them the glory you gave to me, that they may be one as we are one. With me in them and you in me, may they be so completely one that the world will realise that it was you who sent me and that I have loved them as much as you loved me.' For the Man in heaven unity is inseparable from evangelism. For this Man, unity is the indispensable prerequisite for the effective revelation of God's love. Therefore our unity is Jesus' top prayer priority.

The Man in heaven does not much mind if his ministers do or do not wear robes, if service books or spontaneity rule the day, if chanting or tongues is preferred, if women are veiled or vociferous, if his mother or his words are revered, if some bend their knees whilst others straighten their elbows, if some stress this and others emphasise that. But Jesus does mind when those who use service books separate themselves from those who do not, when those who sing in tongues look down on those who do not, when those who genuflect refuse communion to those who do not, when those who favour plain clothes prohibit the robed from their platforms, and so on.

Unity matters to the Man in heaven. The health of his fiancée is at stake. He feels pain as his body slowly dismembers itself. He weeps as he watches the many battalions of his army fight each other in a cruel and silly civil war. And he agonises as his brothers and sisters refuse to speak to each other; his servants feud; his friends dislike one another; his harvesters steal from each other; and his lost children, after gazing in bewilderment at the mayhem, wander off into the camp of the enemy, disenchanted with the King of kings and disbelieving in his divine origin. So Jesus sighs, Satan smiles, unbelievers die, and deceived Christians arrogantly think that God's grace means he approves of their separation, their division and their individualism.

For over ten years I have been involved with a small community called the Ashburnham Stable Family. Its official purpose is 'to encourage the renewal and spiritual unity of all Christian congregations, especially in East Sussex'. During the past ten years a large number of individuals and congregations in East Sussex have embraced spiritual renewal in one way or another. I wish that many more had taken a similar path; nevertheless, congregational life is different from a decade ago. But the last ten years in East Sussex have also been marred by congregational division, disagreement and a marked increase in mutual dislike. If the Ashburnham Stable Family's prayerful encouragement of spiritual renewal appears to have borne some fruit, our encouragement of unity seems to have been totally ineffective.

Many reasons are put forward for the apparent disunity of present-day Christians, but I have come to realise that none of the reasons reach down to the real cause of the disunity. Disunity is caused by individualism, by the emphasis on the self-sufficient individual—personal and congregational—which has tainted the church since the Renaissance. Sermons and books which urge believers to stop being disunited are as impotent as the doctor who tells a patient with a cough to stop coughing. It is not good enough only to analyse the symptoms, the cause must be recognised and treated.

This second part of *The death of Self* trilogy is for those readers of Part One who desire to crucify all their ambition, and wonder what to do with the corpse. This book investigates and stresses both the serious problem of personal and congregational individualism, and the significance and importance of Christian unity. It attempts to learn from the triune God himself; tries to trace and then fathom the mystery which Paul describes in Ephesians 1:9–10; and humbly makes some practical, but scriptural, suggestions about the burial of our individualism. I pray that the words on these pages will help all readers to move from being part of the reason for Jesus' John 17:23 intercession, to becoming part of God's answer to his precious Son's prayer.

The
Oneness of
God

God's undivided, One in Persons Three,
And Three in Inconfused Unity:
Originall of Essence there is none,
'Twixt God the Father, Holy Ghost, and Sonne:
And though the Father be the first of Three,
'Tis but by order, not by entitie.

Robert Herrick

Unity is an over-used word which today means whatever its speaker wants it to mean. Whenever I press people for a synonym the most popular suggestions are words like 'harmony', 'love', 'concord', 'agreement' and 'fraternity'. Roget might agree with them, but the Scriptures do not.

The word 'unity' does not appear very often in the Bible: most translations only use it in Psalm 133 and Ephesians 4. All the other passages which we think are about unity deal with oneness; even the word translated twice in Ephesians 4 as unity is derived from the neuter form of the Greek word for 'one'. Unity is a comfortable, ambiguous word. One is short, sharp and uncompromising. Unity suggests two or three people getting along quite well. One can only mean one. For two to become one they have, in some way, to cease to be two. And that is an uncomfortable notion.

Because the Bible so rarely uses the word unity I suggest that we try to eliminate this unhelpful word from our vocabularies. The Bible does not instruct us to pray for unity, to create unity, or to maintain united relationships. Instead it teaches about oneness, and that is the word which I think we should use. Whenever I use the word unity in this book I don't mean ecumenism, but I have in mind the basic scriptural meaning of 'oneness' or 'being one'.

Many people mistakenly call Jesus' John 17 intercession a prayer for unity. But the Greek word used is *hen*, 'one'. Christ was asking for oneness, not unity; and for a oneness that has the triune God as both its source and its model. 'I pray not only for these, but for those also who through their words will believe in me. May they all be one. Father, may they be one in us, as you are in me and I am in you, so that the world may believe it was you who sent me. I have given them the glory you gave to me, that they may be one as we are one. With me in them and you in me, may they be so completely one that the world will realise that it was you who sent me and that I have loved them as much as you loved me.'

The future Christians prayed for by Jesus have two important features in common: they believe in Jesus, and they come to faith through the words of his disciples. John 20:31 provides a simple statement of faith for future followers: they must believe that Jesus is the Christ, the anointed Messiah, and the Son of God; they also need to believe that Jesus bears the divine name, and that they have received life through that name. Jesus prayed that those who believed, in the sense of personal commitment not intellectual assent, these simple truths would be made one by the Father. No extra doctrinal beliefs are needed for unity; to demand any more is to go beyond Jesus.

In John 17:11 Jesus asks his Father that the disciples 'may be one like us'; and he makes the same request in verses 21–23 for those who will believe in him in the future. In both cases the model for the oneness is the relationship between the Father and the Son; therefore we must examine God himself if we are to understand the nature of our intended unity.

The Jews believed in only one God. Unlike other nations they did not believe in a plurality of gods. Yet the Old Testament contains many hints that the oneness of Yahweh is complex and not single. One of the most popular Old Testament names of God, *Yahweh Sabaoth*, suggests that God is not alone. This name is usually translated 'the Lord of Hosts': it can mean that Yahweh *is* hosts, which would hint at plurality in God's nature, but it is more usually taken to mean that Yahweh *possesses* hosts or armies—which at the very least suggests that God does not exist in heavenly isolation.

The many Old Testament appearances of 'the angel of Yahweh' are significant. This being often appears in human form but is recognised as God himself. Hagar was the first to meet him. In Genesis 16:7–14 she identified him as *El Roi*—the God of Vision; and in Genesis 21:17–19 she heard him speak from heaven—in some way distinct from God, yet at the same time being God. The same thing happened to Abraham, Genesis 22:11–18, and to Jacob, Genesis 31:11–13. Moses met this mysterious being at the burning bush, Exodus 3:1–6, and all the Israelites met him outside Bethel, Judges 2:1–5. These angelic visitations are probably pre-incarnate appearances of Jesus, and are commonly called 'theophanies'. The angel is recognisable as God, yet distinguishable from God: it must have been confusing for the monotheistic Jews.

Most important of all is the first name of God found in the Bible. Genesis 1:1 states, 'In the beginning God...' This is *Elohim*, the name of God which stresses his majesty and omnipotence. The *im* ending means that this is a plural word, yet it takes a singular verb. So really we should say, 'God, they is love'! This happens over 2,000 times in the Old Testament, and is especially clear in Genesis 1:26 where God says, 'Let us make man in our own image, in the likeness of ourselves…' In the Old Testament God is very definitely one, yet mysteriously he is also more than one.

The notion of a God who is one, yet more than one, is developed in the New Testament, but is nowhere defined in terms of a Holy Trinity. The writers simply present information which suggests that both Jesus and the Spirit have a divine nature, without drawing any conclusions from this.

There are passages where the Father, the Son and the Spirit are mentioned together, without any clear structure. Mark 1:9–11; Romans 8; Galatians 4:4–6; 2 Thessalonians 2:13–14; Titus 3:4–6 and Jude 20–21 all link the three in a way that cannot be considered accidental. And there are other passages where the Father, the Son and the Spirit are brought together with a clear structural association. 1 Corinthians 12:3–6; Ephesians 4:4–6; and 1 Peter 1:2 either preface each person with the same adjective or suggest a sequential link.

A deliberate trinitarian formula appears to be used in Matthew 28:19; 2 Corinthians 13:13 and Revelation 1:4, but it is in John's account of Jesus' last supper discourse that the link between the three can be most clearly seen. John 14:16–17, 25–26; 15:26; and 16:13–15 show both the relationship and the distinctiveness of the Father, the Son and the Spirit. The Father sends the Spirit in the name of the Son. But the Son sends the Spirit who issues from the Father. All three are involved in the declaration of truth to man.

John also records the unity of God. The boldest statement is in 10:30, where Jesus' claim, 'The Father and I are one (*hen*)' prompted the Jews to fetch stones to execute him for blasphemy. John 1:1; 8:24,28; 10:38; 14:9–11; and 17:21–23 highlight not the distinctiveness, but the oneness of the Father and the Son. This is a mystery which the New Testament repeatedly states, but nowhere attempts to explain.

The New Testament develops the Old Testament understanding that God is one, but more than one, by clarifying the 'more than one' without weakening the stress that nevertheless he is 'only one'. The 'more than one' is shown to be three, and so today people tend to emphasise that there are three distinctive persons who, in some mysterious way, are united. However, the scriptural stress is slightly, but significantly, different, for the Bible suggests that God is one person whose essence exists in three forms. Our model of Christian unity will be greatly affected by our emphasis in this matter. If we ascribe greater importance to the three distinctive persons of God we will inevitably be more content with the present church situation than if we stress the innate oneness of God.

The Father, the Son and the Spirit are not three distinct individuals, but three self-distinctions within one being. Each form is self-conscious, but does not act independently or in opposition. God is one, he is not divided into three. Yet he reveals his oneness in a threefold diversity of persons, characteristics and functions.

Jesus' intercession in John 17 undoubtedly shows that the oneness of God is the model for contemporary Christian unity, but what this implies is not clear. Some argue that the oneness of God means that organic church union is the only acceptable form of unity. Others state that God's threefold diversity suggests that Christian unity must allow for the reproduction of this diversity in denominational and traditional distinctions. I think that both these positions miss the point: after all, it is improbable that John had the nuances of denominational union in mind when he wrote his gospel! Jesus prayed for oneness so that the world might be given an opportunity to know Jesus' divine origin, and neither intercommunion nor organic union would on their own make one scrap of difference to the world's knowledge of Jesus.

Some say that the intended evangelistic impact of our oneness means that Jesus only desired a common purpose in mission. Others broaden this and say that his prayer is just a request for Christians to work harmoniously together without disagreements. A few argue that, in view of John 14:11–12, it is a unity manifested in miraculous powers. The difficulty with these approaches is that they place the responsibility for creating the relationship on to human shoulders. But the fact that Jesus prays to the Father for oneness presupposes that its origin is in divine action rather than human endeavour: 17:22 shows that Christian unity flows from the Father to the Son to believers. This does not mean believers may be passive, merely that their response is not the source of the relationship.

Most commentators believe that Christian unity is a mystical union which will only be fully seen after the return of Christ, but this is quite unacceptable. Verse 23 says 'may they be so completely one'. The verb is *teleioun* which means that the oneness is absolute, that it is perfected. The NIV unfortunately uses the word unity, but emphasises the degree by accurately rendering it as,

'May they be brought to complete unity.' The verb is passive, which means that Christians are to be made one rather than that they are to make themselves one. And the timescale is temporal rather than eternal. This complete oneness is not something which is reserved for heaven, it is meant to occur in this life so that the world may be effectively challenged about Jesus. The world believes what it sees, and what it sees today is a divided, disagreeing church. Only a visible unity is capable of proving to the world that we are children of the same Father, followers of the same Lord, and partakers of the same Spirit. Evangelistic zeal alone should be enough to make us passionate about unity.

John 17:21–23 states that our unity has to be visible enough to challenge the world to believe in Jesus, and this fact militates against a purely spiritual and mystical union. Jesus' prayer came at the end of his last supper teaching which included, in John 13:34–35 and 15:12–17, the theme of visible love for one another. In 13:35 the consequence of this love is shown to be very similar to the desired result of the intercession in 17:21–23. At the very least this suggests a relationship between sacrificial love and unity, though not necessarily a causal one.

The words of Jesus in John 17:21–23 also show that being one means more than human agreement, fellowship, friendship, common purpose, even sacrificial love; some element of spiritual union, similar to that between the Son and the Father, is demanded. Oneness, or unity, is not simply fraternal harmony, neither is it efficient organisation or common doctrine, though these can bear witness to a pre-existing oneness. The Trinity is not a friendly association of three like-minded, loving, omnipotent persons; the Father, the Son and the Spirit are not just an attractive threesome. No, they is one. They is one in a union of love. And their union demands that we bury our individualism and independence (but not our individuality), for their absolute union is the only acceptable model for Christian unity today.

The Oneness of Israel

When Israel was a child I loved him,
and I called my son out of Egypt.

Hosea

Very few aspects of the Christian faith were sprung on the early church without having been foreshadowed in the Old Testament. From before the beginning God had been unfolding his plan for creation, hinting all along at the final format. Quite often these hints could be fully understood only with the gift of hindsight, but God's passion for unity had been plain from the start.

The account of the creation of mankind points out God's determination to shape human unity in his own divine nature. Genesis 1:26–27 states, 'God said, "Let us make man in our own image, in the likeness of ourselves, and let them be masters of the fish of the sea, the birds of heaven, the cattle, all the wild beasts and all the reptiles that crawl upon the earth." God created man in the image of himself, in the image of God he created them, male and female he created them.' These two verses show that Jesus was not praying for something new in John 17, but for something which had existed at the dawn of time. Mankind was meant to be one from the first moment of human existence; and Elohim themself had been both the source and the model of that original unity.

Some people struggle with the apparent discrepancies between the Genesis 1 and Genesis 2 accounts of creation; especially with the Genesis 1 suggestion that mankind was made in general, as opposed to the Genesis 2 portrayal of the creation of one special man. Yet this is all part of the Elohim mystery. God is one but more than one; therefore it is to be expected that what he creates in his image will also be one, yet more than one. The two creation accounts of Genesis indicate this mystery without attempting to explain it.

However, it is important to note that it is Genesis 1 which states that man is made 'in the image of God himself'. No equivalent claim is mentioned in Genesis 2: Adam is simply 'a man of dust from the soil'. If the phrase 'the image of God' is meant to indicate a physical resemblance, surely it is more likely that it would have been associated with Adam's creation. Again, if the phrase is restricted to the idea of intellect, will and authority surely it would more naturally occur in Genesis 2. The fact that the phrase is only found in Genesis 1 must indicate the important point that the image of God is corporate; and therefore one man on his own—even one man and his wife, or one minister and his congregation—can never truly reproduce the divine image.

Genesis 1 teaches that mankind was made by God to be like God. It was made to be one, but to be more than one; and each person, like each form of God, was meant to be fully self-conscious yet vitally aware of his part in a wider consciousness. Men were not made to be independent, individualistic, or opposed to each other; they were made to exist in a unity which resembles their Creator. Like him, each self-distinction within humanity was given a separate personality, but all men were meant to live in a way which closely resembled the relationship within Elohim themself. God loves individuals and individuality; he loathes individualism.

This mystery is repeated on a smaller scale at Eve's introduction to Adam. The Genesis 2:24 comment, 'This is why a man leaves his father and mother and joins himself to his wife, and they become one body', suggests that the principle of 'one, but more than one' is a basic building block which God intends to be seen at every level of human relationships. The rib incident underlines the fact that although Adam and Eve are to be self-conscious they are not to be independent. The instruction to become one flesh is not only to encourage reproduction but also to remind them that though they have separate personalities they are not to be individualistic, as they have a common source. The best marriages always set an example of oneness which the church should not ignore.

Whether the story about Adam and Eve is literal or parabolic it teaches that all men and all women are, at root, one, and that marriage is a representation and reminder of this deeper unity. I do not believe that married couples are meant to be independent units within mankind, with wedlock an end in itself; rather, partners should be pointers to mankind's basic, and ultimate, oneness. Perhaps this is why I find marriages where the partners are different colours so enchanting.

The emergence of Israel in the Old Testament makes God's passion and pattern for unity particularly clear. Genesis 12:2 records God's promise to Abram, 'I will make you a great nation.' God intended to take one man and make him more than one. Just as all mankind has a oneness in Adam, so God's chosen people were to have a similar oneness in Abram. Abram was to have a miraculously conceived only son who, in his turn, would father the promised nation. But Abram and Sarai foolishly attempted to bring this about by misguided human endeavour: Hagar and Ishmael caused serious long-lasting problems, but they could not ultimately thwart God's purposes. For unity to be true unity 'in the image of God' it must have its source in divine intervention and not in human action.

God gave Israel a tribal structure. There were eleven full tribes (Reuben, Simeon, Levi, Judah, Issachar, Zebulun, Gad, Asher, Benjamin, Dan and Naphtali) and two half tribes (Manasseh and Ephraim), all descended from the twelve sons of Jacob (the half-tribes being descendants of Joseph). With the exception of Levi, when the tribes entered Canaan they were each apportioned a different part of the land. (Some Bibles contain a map at the back showing the allocation of the Promised Land.) The tribes were one, but more than one. Israel was one nation which revealed itself in thirteen distinctive forms, with the emphasis on the one nation rather than on the thirteen tribes—just like their God.

But individualism crept in; tribal loyalties began to be stronger than the national awareness; disputes arose; and gradually the stronger tribes absorbed the weaker ones. Though the tribal distinctions and awareness still remained, Judah became dominant in the south, and Ephraim in the north. Israel was still one nation when Saul became king, but after his death only Judah immediately accepted David. Ishbaal, the son of Saul, was crowned kind of the northern tribes, and seven years of civil war ensued which are recorded in 2 Samuel 2–4. Eventually all the tribes of Israel came to David and, in 2 Samuel 5:1–2, said, 'We are your own flesh and blood...you shall be the leader of Israel.' They acknowledged that their fighting was foolish because, despite their disagreements and differences, they were one nation derived from one flesh.

Israel remained united throughout David's thirty-three year reign and Solomon's early years. But then, in payment for work and materials, Solomon ceded to Tyre Israelite cities in the north-west coastal plain which were part of the tribe of Asher. He also conscripted slave gangs from all the tribes north of Judah. Predictably, this aroused much resentment. When Solomon died the northern tribes insisted on putting their grievances to his son Rehoboam before accepting him as their king. 1 Kings 12 tells the sorry story of division as Rehoboam heeded the advice of those who urged him not to be conciliatory. Schism occurred: the ten northern tribes rebelled, under the leadership of Jeroboam, and established the independent kingdom of Israel. The one nation became two. As far as they were concerned their division was irreconcilable.

For over 300 years the two groupings of tribes fought with each other and with numerous attacking armies from surrounding countries. Each had alternating periods of ascendancy, but eventually both succumbed to invading nations. 2 Kings 17 records the Assyrian conquest of the ten northern tribes of Israel. The two southern tribes of Judah and Simeon held out for another 130 years, but were finally captured by the Babylonians under Nebuchadnezzar (who had previously overrun the Assyrians), and were deported east: 2 Kings 24–25 provides the details. Within 50 years of the fall of Jerusalem the mighty Babylonian empire itself capitulated to Cyrus' Persian army, and another page of God's great mystery unfolded.

God had made Israel one nation from Abram's flesh.

Israel had split itself into two, but what man can divide God can reunite. Isaiah 44:1–45:13 records Isaiah's prophecy, made 170 years before the fall of Jerusalem, that God would use a pagan king to achieve his ends. The story of Ezra, Nehemiah, and the return from exile demonstrates how frequently God uses surprising men and improbable means to bring his people back together. Ezra 1 shows how the mighty Cyrus both initiated and financed the return to Jerusalem. Two of his successors as Persian Emperor, Artaxerxes 1 and Darius, were also crucial to the reshaping of Israel as one nation.

When Israel had been an independent nation in the time of the judges and kings it had been thrusting, aggressive, ambitious, and—to human eyes—very successful, but continually riddled by in-fighting, dazzled by alien gods, polluted by personal and tribal ambition, and so its God-given and God-modelled unity was smashed. After the return from exile Israel was a weak and insignificant vassal state ruled in turn by Persians, Greeks, Ptolemies, Seleucids, Hasmoneans, and finally Romans. Its population was small, its wealth minimal, its influence almost non-existent, but its unity grew and grew. God used the tools of opposition, insignificance and persecution to bring his people back together and back to him. The parallel with the church's present position is striking.

The Old Testament emphasises God's passion for unity by linking it with blessing. Post-exilic Israel was neither as impressive or influential as Israel during the monarchy, but its oneness was far greater. Consequently the blessing it was promised was also larger. This is symbolised by the two temples: Solomon's Temple had been one of the seven wonders of the world, but in Haggai 2:1–9 God promised that he would fill its vastly inferior replacement with a glory and peace which surpassed that of the earlier temple.

No passage in the Old Testament portrays God's love for unity more beautifully than Psalm 133. Perhaps David composed this song immediately after the reunification of Israel and Judah, with seven years of reigning at Hebron still fresh in his mind. If that is so, how wonderful it must have been for him to watch the twelve tribes worshipping instead of fighting. Maybe he wrote it on a hot day as he watched great crowds of people from the different tribes labour up Mount Zion to worship in Jerusalem. Possibly it was the sweat pouring from their foreheads which inspired the imagery.

Whatever or whoever triggered off the psalm is unimportant; these three verses contain much vital information about unity or oneness which must be appreciated and applied today. Verse 1 suggests that unity is morally correct ('good'), aesthetically enjoyable ('pleasant'), and community based ('live together like brothers'). Verse 2 implies that unity is the work of the Holy Spirit ('oil') and mature spiritual leadership ('Aaron's beard'). And verse 3 points to the divine source of unity ('dew') and its relationship with blessing ('where Yahweh confers his blessing, everlasting life'). All of these aspects of unity will be developed in later chapters.

Though Psalm 133 stresses that God is the only source of spiritual unity for man, it also suggests that maintaining such oneness is very hard work. Surely the only link between oil running down the head and dew saturating a mountain top is perspiration pouring off a brow—and nothing speaks more eloquently of effort than sweat.

The Old Testament teaches that only God can create oneness in the first place, and it shows how difficult it is for fallen man to maintain this unity, yet it affirms that human division is not necessarily the end of the story. If out of nothing God can make mankind in his image; if God can keep his promise to Abram despite the mistake with Hagar; if God can restore and reunite Israel despite its division and apparent oblivion in exile; if all these facts, and more, are true, then there surely can be hope that Christ's John 17:23 prayer for today's sorry church may soon be fully answered.

The Example of Jesus

When first mine Infant-Ear
Of Christendom did hear,
I much admir'd what kind of Place or Thing
It was of which the Folk did talk:
What Coast, what Region, what therein
Did mov, or might be seen to walk.
My great Desire
Like ardent fire
Did long to know what Things did ly behind
That Mystic Name, to which mine Ey was blind.

Thomas Traherne

Christian unity pivots on the person and teaching of Jesus. John 1:1 identifies him as the Word who was both with God in the beginning, and yet also was simultaneously God himself. Jesus claims in John 10:30 that he and the Father are one, but John 1:10–11 informs us that when the Word came into the world he was unrecognised by the world and rejected by his own people. In fact Jesus was crucified because the people preferred to believe he was a blasphemous imposter than to believe he was God: his personal unity with God was not apparent to the vast majority of people who met him. Many were impressed by his words, most were challenged in some way about God, some thought the miracles meant he was a prophet; relatively few people realised that this carpenter was the Christ, and even fewer that he shared God's nature.

When the Word became flesh he voluntarily relinquished most aspects of his divinity. He laid down his omnipotence, his omniscience, his omnipresence, and his obvious glory. He could not surrender his divine nature, but he gave up all the unmistakable attributes of that nature. He did not cease to be God, but he no longer looked like God. Jesus' divinity had been instantly recognisable when he had appeared as the angel of the

Lord in the Old Testament, yet in New Testament times, despite his mighty words and works, most people failed to spot his divine nature.

This is vital for our understanding of oneness, for it is this relationship between the Son on earth and the Father in heaven which is the model for contemporary Christian unity. Though in reality the Son and the Father were one, most people perceived them to be two. Though their unity was complete and perfect, it was unconvincing to the casual observer. Though their oneness had existed from before the beginning, it had to be constantly maintained: their unity could only flourish through the Son's continuous communication and fellowship with the Father, and by his complete dependence on the Father.

John's gospel reveals Jesus as one who could do nothing by himself. John 4:34; 5:19, 30; 6:38; 7:28–29; 8:28–29; 10:18; and 12:49–50 all stress the absolute reliance of the Son upon the Father, and this must mean that everything the Son did was a perfect demonstration of his unity with the Father. The Son only said what the Father was saying, only did what the Father was doing, only went where the Father was going. The two could not be divided, so they described themselves as one.

Now although the Son's relationship with the Father is primarily the archetype for all human relationships with the Father, in the context of unity it is also the most important example that we have of the relationship which should exist between Christian believers. We should not, therefore, expect all men to be dazzled by our oneness with other believers, and we should not be surprised by the suggestion that Christians do not appear to be absolutely united. But, like Jesus, we should repeatedly state boldly that we are one, and we should actively maintain our unity by constant communication and fellowship with other believers—and also by our obvious dependence upon them. We who profess to follow the Son should echo his words and behaviour and assert that we can do nothing by ourselves: this means not only that we should depend upon God for direction, guidance, provision and speech, but also that we should all rely on other believers for exactly the same things. We are to be dependent on God, and interdependent with all other believers. There is no room for individualism or independence.

Jesus' relationship with his disciples provides another model for Christian unity. John 1:35–39 suggests that Andrew and John were already disciples of John the Baptist when they were introduced to Jesus. Andrew then took his brother Simon to meet Jesus (John 1:41–42); and Matthew 4:18–22 shows how they—and James and John, another pair of brothers—were finally called by Jesus to leave their work and family to follow him. John 1:43–51 records the calling of Philip and Nathaniel (the Bartholemew of Matthew 10:3). And the calling of Matthew (Levi in Mark and Luke) is detailed by Matthew himself in Matthew 9:9. But each of these summons was a call to follow Jesus, not to be a member of the inner twelve.

Luke 6:12–16 shows how Jesus called together all those who had obeyed his call to forsake everything and follow him, and how, after a night of prayer, he picked out three sets of Galilean brothers, Peter and Andrew, James and John, James and Judas (called Thaddeus by Mark); one pair of friends, Philip and Bartholemew; one unpopular tax-official, Matthew; Thomas the twin; Simon the political activist; and Judas from Kerioth in the Judean hills. These twelve were given a unique double function of community and mission which closely resembles Christ's John 17 prayer for us; Mark 3:13–14 states that Jesus appointed them 'that they might be with him and that he might send them out to preach' (NIV).

The ideal Man was not self-contained. He needed close friends. He needed people to be with him; and his relationship with the twelve adds the vital element of community to our model of unity. Psalm 133 hinted at this, and the relationship between Christ and the twelve almost exactly duplicates the details of that psalm. The twelve were a mixed bunch of young men: most were single, but Peter was married; eleven were from Galilee, with only Judas from Judea; several were fishermen, but Matthew (and possibly Judas/Thaddeus) were taxation officials; James and John were cousins of Jesus (their mother Salome was almost certainly Mary's sister), but the others were unrelated; Simon belonged to an extremist guerilla group working to overthrow the Romans, whilst others earned their living by serving the Romans. And this diverse group of men were selected to be with Jesus, to preach, and, as a direct consequence of this, to be with each other.

The community life of the twelve was unstructured. They had no rules; they lived, laughed, learnt, prayed, travelled, cried, worked and ate together; they listened to each other, disagreed with each other, and had petty jealousies. But these twelve did not exist in isolation, for they were also part of the wider group of Jesus' disciples which numbered several hundred. They had relationships at three different levels: firstly, each disciple was particularly close to another one or two within the twelve, usually their relative and/or partner for mission;

secondly, they were part of the twelve—a group over whose membership they had had no control; and thirdly, they had wider friendships with the whole company of Jesus' followers. The pressures and difficulties they must have experienced in simultaneously maintaining unity in several different directions, as well as developing their own personal relationship with Jesus and the Father, are things that we can relate to with great ease. We need to learn from them: not restricting our relationships to one congregation, but struggling to maintain oneness with a companion, a cell group, a congregation, and all the Christians—whatever their tradition—in our immediate locality, for they are an expression of the world-wide church.

Judas Iscariot is a particularly important member of the twelve for a study on unity or oneness. Judas had been selected by Jesus as the only non-Galilean member of the twelve. He had been entrusted with responsibility for the group's finances in preference to the highly qualified Matthew. He had been a successful preacher; he had experienced God working mighty miracles through his hands; his feet had been washed by Jesus' hands; yet Judas betrayed his master for a pittance.

The point to note is that Jesus maintained his relationship with Judas even after he realised that Judas would betray him. The notion that Jesus had selected Judas from the outset specifically to betray him is unacceptable, for that would mean that Jesus' three year friendship with Judas was a terrible sham. We do not know when Jesus prophetically became aware of Judas' inner turmoil and developing evil intentions, but even at the Last Supper Jesus sought neither to expose Judas publicly, nor to disassociate himself from him: when he announced to the disciples that one of them would betray him they had no idea who it could be.

Matthew 26:49–50 tells what happened in Gethsemane, 'So he [Judas] went straight up to Jesus and said, "Greetings, Rabbi", and kissed him. Jesus said to him, "My friend..."' Only hours before Jesus had taught the disciples that a man can have no greater love than to lay down his life for his friends, and here in the agony of Gethsemane he showed the depths of his love by calling the betrayer his friend. This, to me, is one of the high points of the gospel. It shows how the maintenance of unity was always one of Jesus' highest priorities, but more than that, it deeply challenges many current ideas about church discipline.

We would not have treated Judas in the same way as Jesus. As soon as we thought that he might be stealing from the funds we would have done something about it; at the very least we would have shared our suspicions with another leader. When we realised the magnitude of his intentions surely we would have distanced ourselves from him, perhaps even have ejected him from the twelve. In Gethsemane most of us would have held up a hand to ward off the kiss, and how many would have called Judas 'my friend'—and meant it?

I know what Paul teaches in 1 Corinthians 5, but I beg those who stress and implement this passage in their congregations to include Jesus' treatment of Judas Iscariot in their church discipline equation. Some people argue that Judas was a special case because of the part played by his deed in salvation. But Jesus' arrest did not hinge on Judas' betrayal; our salvation was not dependent on Christ accepting the kiss and calling Judas his friend. No, the central position of Judas in the Easter story is to underline the importance of Jesus' attitude towards him, to magnify God's grace and mercy, and to teach us about love, forgiveness and acceptance in the church.

The Judas episode is not an isolated incident which runs contrary to the main thrust of Jesus' ministry, but is entirely consistent with all his teaching. One parable in particular clearly illustrates Jesus' oft-repeated principle that relationships which have been initiated by God must be maintained—even when it is obvious that one party has been nobbled by Satan!

In the parable of the darnel (Matthew 13:24–30 and 36–43) Jesus tells a typically ridiculous story. His listeners were familiar with fields sown with wheat-seed, and with the problem of darnel weeds growing amongst that wheat. Intelligent farmers diligently weeded out the darnel, yet Jesus' heavenly farmer would rather have unsightly and obvious weeds growing in his field than risk one of his clumsy workers pulling up a single stalk of wheat by mistake. This heavenly farmer claims as his own the responsibility for separating the weeds from the wheat, and he will perform this task of separation only at the final harvest. This parable complements Jesus' teaching in Matthew 7:1–5 and 19:3–9; it is the same principle applied in different areas of life.

The parable of the Last Judgement (Matthew 25:31–46) expands the parable of the darnel by describing in more detail the fundamental separation which will occur at the end of time. We fly in the face of these straightforward parables when we refuse to admit that we are united with some groups of people who profess to follow Christ; when we disassociate ourselves from other groups because of our suspicions; and when we eject people from our group because we feel that they have betrayed their calling. Jesus understood that it was not within his sphere of responsibility to ostracise, condemn, or remove Judas from the ranks of the twelve. He knew that he should leave the weeding of Satan's seedlings to his Father, and that it was unlikely the divine weeding would begin before the end of time.

This principle is applied practically in Luke 9:49–50. The twelve had seen a man successfully exorcising in Jesus' name, and, because he was not a member of the inner twelve, had tried to stop him. Jesus told John, 'You must not stop him: anyone who is not against you is for you.' It is likely that the man had not been authorised by Jesus, but because he was not opposed to the twelve Jesus instructed them to treat him as one who was on their side.

Some assert that this saying is contradicted by Jesus' words in Luke 11:23, but they fail to recognise the fundamental difference between the two verses. Luke 11:23 is not the inverse of 9:50. It is addressed to outsiders, not disciples; and it warns them that it is impossible for them to be neutral towards Jesus himself. But Luke 9:50 is addressed to disciples, not outsiders, and it warns them not to disregard or oppose those who profess to be working in Jesus' name but are not part of their own immediate group. These words condemn the siege mentality of some Christian groups, the competitive independence of many congregations, the arrogant intolerance of others. All of these groups need to heed the words of Jesus and embrace all who profess to serve Jesus—especially those who serve him in a way different from their own.

Jesus was passionate about oneness. He maintained

his own united relationship with the Father, even in the torment of his struggle with the Father's will on the Mount of Olives (Luke 22:39–44). He called hundreds to follow him, and those who responded discovered that, as part of the package, they had to love their fellow followers in the same sacrificial manner that they were loved by Christ. He selected a varied group of young men to be his close companions and gently moulded them into a cohesive unit: their experience of unstructured community life would provide the pattern for the church's future.

Jesus taught the twelve to maintain their united relationships by depending absolutely on God, and to show this by practising self-denial in their rejection of office, status and ambition. He instructed them in the way of oneness by loving, embracing and accepting Judas; by teaching them not to weed out Satan's plants; by correcting their intolerance towards those who were not part of their own group; by abundantly blessing the Luke 10 seventy-two disciples; and by helping the twelve to grasp that they were only a small part of a much larger group of equally valuable and important followers.

Finally, in John 17:11, he prayed that they might be one in the same way that he was one with the Father; and then he went on to pray that this oneness would be repeated in the lives of all those who came to believe in him through the disciples' words. Jesus' prayerful, persistent, and practical passion for unity still exists. We know that he wants us to be perfectly one, so why do we find oneness so unpalatable? We know that he says our unity will cause the world to be effectively challenged about him, so why do we seek other means to achieve this goal? We know that he urges us to accept those who serve him in other traditions and denominations, so why do we deliberately disobey his clear teaching? We know that he prays for our oneness, so why do we resist his fervent intercession? Surely the reproduction and application of his passion for Christian oneness must become a very high priority in our prayers, in our preaching, and in our practical living?

The Origin of Oneness

Don't touch me.
Don't question me.
Don't speak to me.
Stay with me.

Samuel Becket

Paul's letter to the Ephesians has been described as the Gospel of Unity. It was written about thirty years after the birth of the church, most likely when Paul was under arrest in Rome. The title 'Ephesians' is slightly misleading because, unlike Paul's other letters, it was probably written as a circular letter to the whole church, rather than to the believers in one location in order to deal with their particular problems. Its intended general readership, and its composition late in Paul's life, make it especially significant.

In this letter Paul passes on Christ's passion for oneness, and explains in detail how the church has been made innately one, but more than one. The central statement of Ephesians is in 1:23 where the church is described as, 'the fullness of him who fills the whole creation'. This phrase encapsulates the two complementary ideas of Paul which are basic to any understanding of Christian unity: that the church is simultaneously both 'in Christ' and is 'the body of Christ'. We will be examining these ideas in the next chapter.

Ephesians 1:3–14 is Paul's description of spiritual blessing, and verses 4–14, which catalogue seven blessings, expound on Paul's phrase in verse 3: 'all the spiritual blessings of heaven in Christ'. In most epistles Paul lists seven spiritual ideas, and usually follows the Jewish menorah by including the most important in the sequence as fourth in the list: it thus becomes the central support on which the other six hang. The fourth in this list of seven blessings is found in verses 9 and 10, 'He has let us know the mystery of his purpose, the hidden plan he so kindly made in Christ from the beginning to act upon when the times had run their course to the end: that he would bring everything together under Christ, as head, everything in the heavens and everything on earth.'

The fourth blessing reveals the main theme of Ephesians: creation will be renewed by Christ who will reunite all its parts into one organism, with himself as head. These two verses, together with Colossians 1:17–20, suggest that oneness in Christ is God's ultimate purpose not just for all mankind, but for all creation. In these verses Paul looks forward longingly to what will happen at the end of time, but in Ephesians 2:11–22 he describes an aspect of unity which has already taken place. Perhaps the present oneness in Christ of believers, whatever their race, is a foreshadowing of the future mysterious oneness in Christ of all creation.

All of the Ephesians 1 blessings have been formulated since before the beginning of time; but even though they can now be experienced in part, they must wait until the end of the world before they can be fully realised. Paul concedes that this is a mystery, but considers that God's revelation of his eternal intention is a crucial spiritual blessing. It is hard for us today to understand Paul's teaching on our future oneness with all creation, as hard as it must have been for Jews in Paul's day to grasp that God had made them one in Christ with Gentiles. But just because this blessing is difficult to comprehend it does not mean we are justified in ignoring it. I believe it is important that we fully grasp the significance of this blessing, and even more vital that we diligently demonstrate its reality to the world.

A straightforward reading of this Ephesians mystery refutes any idea of an exclusively individualistic salvation and independent Christian living. The mysterious ultimate purpose of God is not to amass the largest possible number of redeemed individuals into his heaven, but to fill heaven with one being. The shepherd did not seek his lost sheep just because it might have been in danger (though it was), but because his one flock was depleted. The woman did not hunt for her lost drachma just because it was valuable to her (though it was), but because her total savings were incomplete. The forgiving father did not treat his lost son to a personal celebration (though he was specially honoured), instead he gave the whole family a party. Jesus has not saved me just so that I can go to heaven (though I will), but to unite me in himself with his redeemed creation, thus making me a very small part of one new organism, of which he is head. Our destiny is to be eternally one, but more than one: to be one in Christ with all creation, yet simultaneously to retain our individuality.

Politicians divide between those who emphasise the importance of the individual and those who stress the priority of the state. The Bible presents these as parallel truths to be embraced, rather than as opposites to be argued about. It ascribes infinite worth to every single person, but also presents absolute oneness as both the inescapable future destiny and the intended present-day reality for all these highly prized men and women.

In Ephesians 2:11–22 Paul explains the origin of this

unity, showing that though Jews and Gentiles were once hopelessly divided, their reconciliation with each other has now been made possible by Christ's death on the cross. Verses 13–16 are critical; in them Paul writes as a Jew to Gentile Christians: 'But now in Christ Jesus, you that used to be so far apart from us have been brought very close, by the blood of Christ. For he is the peace between us, and has made two into one and broken down the barrier which used to keep them apart, actually destroying in his own person the hostility caused by rules and decrees of the Law. This was to create one single New Man in himself out of the two of them and by restoring peace through the cross, to unite them both in a single Body and reconcile them with God.'

Unity is not a nice idea which exists only in the minds of armchair romantics, it's a blood-stained reality which was born on a wooden cross. Christ died to make us one: one with God and one with each other; and we dare not be so dishonest as to claim the benefit of the God-ward union while ignoring the demands of the man-ward union. Even the shape of the cross points towards a reconciliation by Christ's blood which is both vertical and horizontal. Romans 5:9–11 emphasises our reconciliation with God, and Ephesians 2:11–22 stresses our human reconciliation with each other. Surely passages like these, which are central to our understanding of salvation, demand that we bury all our personal and congregational individualism and independence. The way into the Christian life may be undoubtedly personal, but the Christian way of life is meant to be unashamedly corporate.

In Romans 5 Paul speaks about *our* reconciliation rather than *my* reconciliation, and in Ephesians 2:16 he boldly puts the creation of horizontal human oneness before our vertical divine reconciliation. The twelve disciples had been personally called to follow Jesus, and only later discovered that one implication of this was their community life together. But in Ephesians 2:16 Paul states that the death of Christ first unites us all in one body, and only then reconciles that one body with God.

There may be an eschatological hint here of the great union between Christ and his bride at the heavenly wedding. But Ephesians 2:16 clearly shows why our united relationships with other believers are so important: oneness does not just facilitate evangelism, it does not just glorify God, it is not only an obedient response to Christ's clear command, it is also a vital aspect of our reconciliation with God, for on the cross Christ made us one to reconcile us with God. This explains the New Testament passion for oneness, and is in stark contrast to the common contemporary picture of an exclusively individualistic reconciliation with God.

Paul writes about oneness as an established fact: in verse 15 he describes something which has taken place. The work of reconciliation is finished. The one single new man has been created. We have been united in a single body. Just as we must respond to Christ's love to receive our reconciliation with God, so too we must respond in faith to receive our reconciliation with other men and women. And just as we are ambassadors of our divine reconciliation and are called to live in the good of this in a manner which encourages others to receive the benefits of Calvary, so too we are meant to live in the reality of our cross-forged Christian oneness in a way that challenges others to believe all the things Jesus mentioned in John 17:21–23. Those who pray 'Father make us one' express their disbelief in the finished work of the cross. Since Calvary we only need pray, 'Father help us to live as one.'

Christ's Single Body

*The body of Christ should be a powerful testimony
to the reality of the risen Christ today. That will be
true only when individual christians, or groups of
christians, lose their independence and learn again
what it means to belong to one another and to share
together their common life in Christ.*

David Watson

In recent years there has been a considerable emphasis on the New Testament teaching about the body of Christ. Yet I think that a distorted idea has been popularised, with thousands of ministers teaching their congregations that they are the body of Christ. This has resulted in the absurd, perhaps even blasphemous, belief that in any small town there can be half-a-dozen, or more, different bodies of Christ. True, Matthew 18:20 states that Christ is personally present in any and every small gathering of believers. But the presence of Christ in a congregation is no reason for defining it as the body of Christ, or for any congregation claiming to itself the New Testament teaching about the body.

The body is Paul's most vivid image of the church. In Romans 12:4–8 he states that the body includes himself, his fellow-workers, his readers, and Christ. He does not say, 'You are the body.' He does not even say, 'You are a body.' Instead he posits a union which, at the very least, embraces Christ in heaven, his readers in Italy (Romans 16:1–16 implies several different congregations), and his team—wherever they may be. The image of the body suggests a living, purposeful unity, and rejects dull uniformity. Just as God is one, but more than one, so the church is one, but with many parts. Just as

God has three self-conscious and distinctive forms, so the church has many self-conscious, interdependent members. 'All of us, in union with Christ, form one body, and as parts of it we belong to each other.' Clearly, although it is made up of individual parts, there is no room for individual self-sufficiency in the body.

In 1 Corinthians 10:17, having defined the loaf as Christ, Paul says: 'Though there are many of us, we form a single body because we all share in this one loaf.' Again, the 'one, but more than one' idea is used; again, the body is defined as more than the congregation reading the letter; and, again, the essential oneness of Christ's followers is stressed, this time with a eucharistic emphasis.

Paul develops the image in Ephesians by identifying the church as the body of Christ. In 1:22–23 he names Christ as 'head of the Church; which is his body'. In 2:15–16 he stresses that there is 'one single New Man' and 'a single Body'. In 4:4–5 he lists seven 'ones', and the first is 'one Body', seen in 4:12 to be the 'Body of Christ'. This section of Ephesians underlines 1:3–14 by showing that, though oneness exists in Christ and can be experienced here and now, there is still another element to be realised: 'In this way we are all to come to unity in our faith and in our knowledge of the Son of God, until we become the perfect Man, fully mature with the fullness of Christ himself.' Finally, in Ephesians 5:23–30 Paul shows again that the church is Christ's body 'and we are its living parts'.

He mentions this teaching in Colossians 1:17–18, repeats it in 1:24, and reminds his readers in 3:15 that they have been called together only as parts of one body. In all these passages Paul applies the body metaphor only to the universal church, and never to a single congregation. This has enormous implications for unity, for whenever a congregation considers itself to be either the body or a body of Christ, it has no reason to bother about its relationships with other local congregations. But when a congregation has been correctly taught that it is only part of the one body, and is therefore interdependent with all other parts, passages like Ephesians 4:16 come alive with their original meaning and are naturally applied across the local traditional and denominational divides. If we think that *our* congregation is a body we will become an individualistic, independent group, but if we know that we are only a small part of the one body we will have to bury our congregational individualism if we are to keep our spiritual integrity intact.

For centuries believers have primarily understood the word 'church' to mean a building. Catholics have always thought of the church essentially as a denomination; and more recently evangelicals have thought of the church in terms of a congregation. Yet when they all get away from their buildings, their congregations and their denominations, at large events like Mission England and Spring Harvest, they instinctively recognise that the church is nothing to do with their building, congregation or denomination but is much, much bigger, and that the church is innately one.

1 Corinthians 12:27 is the only 'body' passage which can possibly be stretched to a plausible local application. But because 1 Corinthians 12 is such a popular passage Paul's words here, 'you together are Christ's body' have been lifted out of their context and given undue emphasis; and so the popular view has been established that the body teaching is primarily of congregational application.

However, this verse is set in the context of the two eucharistic passages 10:14–22 and 11:17–32 which stress the oneness in Christ of the whole church. Paul shows that this universal oneness must be applied in a geographic area by the absence of factions, and one of his main reasons for writing 1 Corinthians is to urge the different factions in Corinth to come together.

1 Corinthians 12:27 also follows on from 12:12 where Paul argues that the way a human body gives unity to all its component parts is the way Christ gives unity to all Christians in his body: verse 13 is another one of Paul's 'we' passages. And what he says in verses 14–30 is so similar to Romans 12:3–8 that I find it difficult to understand how anybody who has read more of Paul than 1 Corinthians 12 can ever suggest that any single congregation is a body of Christ.

Some people argue that the body metaphor must be applied congregationally because in the universal body the most each of us can ever consider ourselves to be is one microscopic cell in a layer of subcutaneous flab. But that is exactly the point of the metaphor! We are only a very small part of one body. Others take Paul literally and suggest that his description of an eye, an ear, and a leg presumes a congregational application, as only there can an individual be so significant. But Paul's purpose in these verses is to stress that Christ is the head, and the references to an eye and an ear are in order to teach that no man should aspire to such self-importance. His use of the hand, foot, and unmentionable parts are graphic illustrations of the fact that no congregation should ever consider itself to be independent and omnicompetent in a locality.

The extent of the popular misunderstanding about the

body is matched only by that of the mistake about our relationship with Christ. While the scriptural thrust is overwhelmingly that we are 'in Christ', most individuals have been taught to turn that upside down and proudly state that 'Jesus lives in my heart'. It is a matter of emphasis. The New Testament contains over fifty verses which describe believers as in Christ, in Jesus, in God, in Christ Jesus, or in the Lord. They include such important verses as Romans 6:11; 2 Corinthians 5:17; Galatians 3:27–28; Ephesians 5:8; Philippians 2:1–2; Colossians 3:3; and 1 Thessalonians 2:14. However only Romans 8:10; 2 Corinthians 13:5; Galatians 2:20; Ephesians 3:17; and Colossians 1:27 suggest that Jesus is in us. And of these Ephesians 3:17 refers to a future corporate indwelling which we are not yet strong enough to endure; Romans 8:10 is surrounded by verses which emphasise that we are in Christ and the Spirit is in us; and in four the 'you' is plural rather than singular.

To note this is not merely to play with prepositions. My understanding about my relationship with Jesus inevitably affects my thinking about unity. I know that the oneness of God means that if the Spirit is in me then so too are the Father and the Son. The 'in Christ' and 'Christ in us' verses are complementary, not contradictory. But we should reflect, not reverse, the scriptural stress in this matter. If I emphasise that Jesus is in me I am bound to think of myself as an important, independent, individual; almost as someone bigger than Jesus. But if I know that I am in Jesus I will be convinced that he is larger than me; and I will also realise that there must be countless others who are together with me, in him. The scriptural stress of 'all one in Christ Jesus' reminds me of my essential cross-made and Christ-centred unity. Whereas the human emphasis on 'Jesus in me' encourages self-sufficient individualism.

The two ideas of the body and our corporate indwelling of Christ are not the only New Testament pictures which underline the innate oneness of all believers. Ephesians 5:21–33 suggests that the husband-wife relationship is analogous to that between Christ and the whole church; both this passage, and 2 Corinthians 11:2, introduce the idea of the church as Christ's bride. But Christ is not polygamous. He only wants one wife, and so even this picture hints at ultimate union in and with him.

Paul's other picture is of the church as a building. In Ephesians 2:19–22 Paul informs his readers that they are 'part of a building'. There is only one building, but it has several parts; and the function of the entire building is to be the dwelling place of God. Christ is the main cornerstone of this building, and it is the cornerstone which keeps the walls together, and prevents the building from falling apart.

Throughout the New Testament the message is repeatedly rammed home that the church is one. Tiny groups of believers scattered across Asia and Europe were reminded that they were only part of Christ's body, only part of God's building, only part of the Son's bride. They were taught to think of themselves as having been brought together by Christ, to be united with all other congregations and believers to God. They were one. They did not have to pray that God would make them one because they had been made one by Christ's death on the cross. However, there were stresses and strains.

At first the Greeks thought that their widows were being overlooked in the daily distribution of resources. Later on the Jewish Christians were unsure whether they should accept hospitality from the new Gentile converts. As the faith spread further round the Mediterranean so sectarianism began to emerge. To counter this, the New Testament is packed with practical advice for individuals and congregations about how their unity could, and should, be maintained. For just as the Son had to maintain his united relationship with the Father, so our Christ-forged oneness with all other believers needs continually to be nourished and sustained.

Maintaining Oneness

The call to Christian unity is constantly regenerated in us by eagerness to conform to the Gospel. By its insistence on love for all men, the Gospel cannot tolerate our remaining in a state of hostility towards other Christian bodies.

Roger Schutz

The early church began by following the pattern of community life set by Christ and the inner twelve. Acts 2:42–47 shows how the 3,000 Pentecost converts remained faithful to the apostles' teaching, the eucharist, prayer, and each other. And it was this commitment to each other which was vital in maintaining the unity which Christ had made on the cross. They demonstrated this commitment by selling some of their assets and distributing the proceeds to those in particular need, by generously sharing their food, and by participating in daily corporate prayer at the Temple and in frequent eucharistic services at each other's homes.

Acts 4:32 describes the, by then, 5,000 strong church in these impressive terms, 'the whole group of believers was united, heart and soul'; and gives as evidence the fact that, 'no one claimed for his own use anything that he had, as everything they owned was held in common'. Clearly they had buried their individualism. It is interesting to note the evangelistic impact of this unity: Acts 2:47 states, 'Day by day the Lord added to their community those destined to be saved.' Acts 4:33 adds, 'they were all given great respect'. This Acts 4 community was almost entirely contained in Jerusalem. Today also there are rarely more than 5,000 believers in any one geographic area, so we must believe that it is possible for all the believers in a town or rural area today to maintain their true oneness by this sort of united lifestyle.

The first threat to the oneness of the early church came in Acts 6:1. Greek-speaking Jews worshipped in different synagogues from Hebrew-speaking Jews, and it would have been easy, perhaps obvious, for the church to follow Judaism and divide into two self-administrating groups based on language. But maintaining unity was so important that seven deacons were elected to solve the food allocation and distribution problem. In 1 Corinthians 6:1–8 Paul rebuked his readers for not taking equally practical action to settle a dispute between two believers.

The first major issue which the early church had to resolve was whether they would accept Gentile converts, indeed whether Gentiles could be converts. Acts 10:1—11:18 relates how God convinced Peter both that salvation was for the Gentiles, and that he should breach Jewish tradition by accepting Gentile hospitality. Paul repeatedly spells out how, in Christ, Jew and Gentile are now one. But though this was accepted, there were still radical differences over hospitality. In Galatians 2:11–14 Paul reports on his face-to-face confrontation with Peter: Paul believed that by eating exclusively with Jewish Christians Peter was suggesting that only converted Jews were true Christians. This was threatening to produce two separate communities who never met, not even to share the eucharist. Paul knew that Peter believed Gentiles could be saved, even though his behaviour denied this, and Paul would not countenance such divisive cowardice.

So what would Paul say to our leaders today? What

would he say to those neighbouring congregations which never share communion? We may believe they are Christians, but by never breaking bread with them our behaviour is as questionable as Peter's. Oneness is not maintained in a committee meeting or special service, but at a meal table, as couples who worship in different buildings yet live in the same street eat together.

The persecution after Stephen's death caused the gospel to spread far beyond Jerusalem. Acts 11:21–30 shows how the leaders travelled widely to encourage the small groups of believers and to preserve their relationships. Verse 29 reveals one practical way of maintaining oneness across the gaps of culture and distance: the Gentile Christians gave as much money as they could to help their Jewish brothers.

Romans 12:13; 1 Corinthians 16:1–4; and 2 Corinthians 8:1–15 all stress the need for inter-church giving, yet today's Baptists generally support the Baptist Missionary Society, Anglicans usually give to an Anglican-based missionary society, Restorationists normally finance their own projects, and so on. Some prosperous suburban churches have 'twinned' with struggling inner city churches or 'adopted' a congregation in a foreign country (it's easier to feel one with Christians who live a long way away), but these links rarely make any contribution to visible unity as they are usually within the same tradition and denomination. When will an English Baptist church support a third world independent Black pentecostal church? When will there be a heap-offering at Downs or Dales Bible Week for an evangelical Anglican or Methodist project? When will the Spring Harvest and Keswick collections be sent to Mother Teresa's work? When will we maintain our true oneness in Christ by giving inter-church aid across our man-made boundaries? The very name 'Christian' originated among the generous Acts 11 believers in Antioch; if we are to merit their label then surely we should imitate their behaviour.

The financial gifts that they received must have dramatically underlined to the Judean Christians both that they were part of one, much bigger, body, and that they were interdependent with all these other congregations. Romans 12:3–13; 1 Corinthians 12:4–30; and Ephesians 4:1–16 all emphasise both the interdependence and the variety of Christian congregations. We must learn to apply these passages so that the gifts and ministries referred to effectively build up the one body of Christ, rather than apply them in a way which encourages congregational isolation and independence. The variety inherent within the one body already exists in every town and area; all that we lack are a vital appreciation of, and practical commitment to, all other congregations.

Paul urged his readers to do everything possible to maintain oneness. But in particular he pressed them not to do six things which harm the one body, and to do six things which build it up.

Romans 3:27 states that there is now no room for boasting. The one body is badly hurt whenever an individual, congregation or denomination boasts of its growth, its achievements, its blessing and so on. 1 Corinthians 1:29—3:23 stresses that we have nothing to boast about, because it is God alone who makes things grow. The congregation which boasts of now having 500 members is as ridiculous as the teenager who boasts of being six feet tall or the big toe that boasts of being longer than its neighbour. In 2 Corinthians 11:30 Paul says, 'If I am to boast, then let me boast of my own feebleness.' We should emulate him.

1 Corinthians 4:5 states that there must be no prejudging. In Acts 9:26 Paul had been at the receiving end of an inaccurate premature judgement, so he knew how destructive this is. Yet today we often dismiss ministers and members of other local congregations without any basis for our opinions except bigotry and arrogance. Our presumptions about neighbouring Christians are normally as absurd as the thumb which maligns the ear, just because it does not move. We declare our rejection of God-ordained variety and distinctiveness within the one body when we think or suggest that members of other congregations would be better off if they joined us. If the head highly values all the other organs, then so should we—and our congregational behaviour should correspond to our beliefs.

Romans 14:1; Philippians 2:13; 2 Timothy 2:24; and Titus 3:9 all stress that there are to be no arguments. So we argue. We delight to get caught up in disagreements about doctrine, wrangles about worship, struggles about structure, and disputes with other denominations. We arc convinced that we are right and that they are wrong. We are sure that they will be greatly helped if only we can get them to agree with us. We choose to disregard Paul's words.

1 Corinthians 1:10–16 and 3:4 state that there must be no personality cults. 'What could be more unspiritual than your slogans. "I am for Paul" and "I am for Apollos"?' Yet we support particular individuals and criticise others. Successful pastors and evangelists create societies around themselves, seeking supporters and backers. Some people revere the Pope, whilst others

deem him Antichrist; some venerate John Wimber, others consider him heretical; some applaud the Bishop of Durham, and others endlessly malign him. In our congregations, our areas, our denominations and our traditions we divide over personalities, and in so doing we try to chop limbs off Christ's one body.

Galatians 5:16–26 states that there is to be no self-indulgence; and it equates feuds, factions, disagreements and quarrels with fornication, sorcery, drunkenness and orgies. All of these sins are different manifestations of self-indulgence, and all are equally damaging to the one body. Verse 26 adds, 'We must stop being conceited, provocative and envious.'

And Ephesians 4:31 states that we are not to hold grudges, but instead we are to be friends. But we do hold grudges, we do remember what he said, she did, and they alleged. We are still livid that ten years ago that lot down the road poached twenty of our young people, and we seethe whenever another Christian who has moved into the area joins the big church in the centre of town without having tried our small congregation. Why do we not listen to Paul? Why do we not perceive the damage we do to the body? Why do we prefer division and individualism to unity?

Paul's six tips for maintaining oneness sound weak today. They do not appear to be in tune with the spirit of this age, but they are in step with the Holy Spirit. In Romans 15:5–6 and Philippians 4:5 he urges 'be tolerant': tolerance is very closely related to grace. God is exceedingly tolerant with us; and he calls us not to be pharisaically pernickety with each other, but lovingly to put up with each other's doctrinal and behavioural idiosyncrasies.

In Philippians 2:3–8 he commands us 'to be self-effacing'. This is the essence of God: the Father remains invisible, the Son took the form of a human servant, and the Spirit lives to give glory to the others. We do not like this. We wish God was different, and sometimes our hymns and sermons suggest that he is. But we are called to be self-effacing, not self-asserting. Most vital body organs are only seen when there has been an accident. Some churches think that unity is maintained by inviting other congregations to their own activities. But the godly self-effacing way is to go and silently sit in others' services, without expecting a special greeting in the notices, and without telling somebody about our humility.

In Ephesians 5:21 Paul demands, 'Give way to one another in obedience to Christ.' This is the outward result of inner self-effacement. This discipline of submission is central to our faith. We argue, manoeuvre and fight to get our own way. Ministers surround themselves with men who can be relied upon to agree with them. But we have to learn that nothing matters that much. God rarely imposes his will on us; therefore, instead of imposing our will on others we should graciously give way to each other—in obedience to Christ.

Acts 15:3–4 reports how the news of pagan conversions elsewhere was received 'with the greatest satisfaction' in Phoenicia and Samaria. Because we are part of one body we should similarly rejoice when we hear that a neighbouring congregation of a different tradition is growing, and lament when a nearby congregation divides or struggles. A minister experiences revival, not only when his congregation suddenly increases in size, but also when his remains static while a neighbouring congregation from an opposite tradition unexpectedly triples, and he responds with sheer unadulterated delight. Yet such is the spirit of competition within us that jealousy and smugness sometimes surface in our midst. We belittle the achievements of others; and on hearing bad news say, 'We knew it would happen.'

In 1 Corinthians 11:28 we are instructed to recollect our attitude to the body before receiving the sacraments. 2 Corinthians 10:7 states, 'Face plain facts. Anybody who is convinced that he belongs to Christ must go on to reflect that we all belong to Christ no less than he does.' The glorious passage about oneness in Ephesians 2:11–22 is prefaced by 'do not forget'. We must regularly remind ourselves, and certainly remind ourselves before every communion service, that there is only one body, that Christ has a single bride, that the Father is building just one temple, and that our congregation is only a small and insignificant part of the church. We must stop equating the church with our congregation: the universal church is so much more than the sum total of all congregations, and the local church is unlikely ever to be a single congregation. In recent years both evangelicals and charismatics have increasingly been caught up in the false cult of the congregation, with its ridiculous pressure to genuflect towards the largest congregations. The local church is the church in the locality, and is made up of all the believers who live in that locality—wherever and however they worship. And whenever they worship they need to be reminded by their leaders about the oneness of the body.

Finally, Paul exhorts all Christ's followers to live in love and peace. 1 Corinthians 13 emphasises the priority of love. 2 Corinthians 13:11; Galatians 5:13–15; Ephesians 4:3–16; Colossians 3:12–15; and 1 Thessalonians

5:14 all stress the need to live in peace, and associate this in some way with unity. We have to confess that we do not find this easy.

In most towns and villages today the Christian church appears to be hopelessly divided. In some places there is open antagonism, in others silent tension, and in many more apathy rules the day. Yet this should not be so. We are one. Christ has made us one. His John 17:21 prayer has been answered. At the cross Jew and Gentile, black and white, rich and poor, Anglican and Baptist, Catholic and Protestant, evangelical and liberal, charismatic and pentecostal all were brought together into a Single Man in order that they might be brought to the Father. As we have seen, since Calvary there has been no need for us to pray, 'Father make us one.'

But the world does not believe in Jesus' divine origin, it does not realise that Jesus was sent by the Father, it is not being challenged by the oneness of the church, for we are not visibly one. Jesus has made us one—he is in the Father and we are in him—but we seldom receive this from him, we rarely recognise what he has done, and even less frequently do we assume our responsibility for maintaining our Christ-forged unity.

Honest and effective preaching, supernatural signs and wonders, prayerful and sacrificial living, all of these are important in communicating the good news; but in the glorious God-given task of local and world-wide evangelisation very few things matter as much as maintaining the oneness of the church.

Visible
Oneness
Today

Almighty God,
you have knit together your elect
into one communion and fellowship
*   in the mystical body of your Son.*
Give us grace so to follow your blessed saints
in all virtuous and godly living,
that we may come to those unspeakable joys
which you have prepared for those who truly love you;
through Jesus Christ our Lord.

Collect for All Saints' Day in the
Church of England's Alternative Service Book.

It appears to me that oneness is neither an evangelical nor a charismatic priority. For the last quarter of a century thinking and experimentation about unity have mainly been the preserve of the liberal arm of the one body. Unfortunately their discussions have centred on the red herring of organic union, with the net result of widespread disenchantment and disastrous denominational mergers. Consequently evangelicals have tended to associate oneness with the ecumenical movement; and because this is, to them, indelibly linked with heresy, talk of unity has come to be treated with grave theological suspicion.

In the early days of charismatic renewal the activities of organisations like the Fountain Trust and Crusade for World Revival meant that spiritual renewal was accidentally intertwined with unity. Fresh life in the Spirit went hand in hand with discovering and appreciating long-lost brothers and sisters. The very first song of the charismatic movement was 'We are one in the Spirit, we are one in the Lord'. And who can forget the impact of 'Come together'? But those days have long gone. There are now so many charismatic ministers within every tradition and denomination that few need cross ecclesiastical boundaries to enjoy charismatic fellowship. Groups like

Mainstream, GEAR and Anglicans for Renewal do outstanding work within their respective denominations, but their very existence presumes that unity has a much lower priority than renewal. Even the song 'We are one in the Spirit' is no longer to be found in any of the current charismatic chorus-books.

Yet it seems to me that God has been drawing the attention of his church to his strong feelings about this matter. I know that many sinners have been saved in evangelistic campaigns like Mission England, but for most participants the lasting memory of Mission England is the unity experienced with other saints: tragically, this is only a memory. I know that many clergy were helped by John Wimber's Signs and Wonders Weeks, but the greatest miracle was the astonishing mixture of ministers attending. Sadly, this mixture is also now only a memory.

At the 1974 Lausanne International Congress on World Evangelism two men rose to brief fame. Howard Snyder spoke on the church as God's agent of evangelism, and Juan Carlos Ortiz taught about church unity. Snyder urged Christians to see themselves as the community of God's people and not as members of an organisation. Ortiz preached his famous 'we are called to be mashed potato' sermon. Both men were widely criticised. Snyder's words on structure were applauded and seized upon, but his pleas for community were ignored. Ortiz's ideas about Lordship were devoured, but his thoughts on discipleship were distorted, and his pleas for oneness fell on deaf ears. If, instead of a field of potatoes becoming one huge bowl of mash, he had used the analogy of many separate ingredients becoming one gigantic Christmas pudding surely nobody would have had any emotional or exegetical grounds for faulting him? Most western Europeans were so repulsed by the inherent blandness and sameness of mashed potato that they missed the essential point of his parable.

Ten years later the same thing happened to John Wimber. In 1984 at Westminster God used the commendation of the recently dead David Watson to draw House Church, Baptist, Methodist, Catholic and Anglican charismatic leaders together for the first time since the demise of the Fountain Trust. Wimber's teaching about signs and wonders was widely absorbed, but his passionate pleas for unity were almost entirely ignored. The following year John Wimber spoke at two conferences: at Wembley the audience was almost entirely Anglican and Baptist; at Brighton it was predominately House Church.

I believe that the Scriptures suggest that few things matter as much as our oneness, and I think that at Lausanne and Westminster God was drawing the attention of evangelicals and charismatics to his concern. The heart of the gospel is reconciliation, and unity is its essential expression. To be passionate about the gospel yet half-hearted about oneness is to be inconsistent. The mystery which God unfolded at Calvary was that in Christ he wanted to make one New Man, and bring him to himself. To press on in congregational isolation, collecting individual converts in the way Red Indians once collected scalps, is to work contrary to God's clear revelation.

I suggest that we must allow God's priority to become our passion, and if this is to happen I believe there are several practical steps which need to be taken. We must frequently and openly acknowledge that unity is God's present purpose for the church, and then we must align our personal and congregational actions with our words. We must go on publicly confessing that our individualism, our competitiveness and our needless duplication are intrinsically sinful, and we must continually encourage our colleagues to point out to us when we slip into old independent, isolationist, individualistic attitudes.

We must stop our relentless public criticism of those who believe that Jesus is the Christ, who believe that he is the Son of God, who believe that he is divine, who believe that they have received eternal life through his name, but who also believe many other things with which we profoundly disagree. If Jesus has prayed that all who believe these four truths will be completely one, our refusal to stand together with some of those who subscribe to these truths must be sin. Even the pagans unite with those they agree with.

We must demonstrate our disdain for man-made boundaries by regularly climbing over them and attempting to dismantle them. Those ministers who share Christ's passion for unity will open their pulpits to speakers from other traditions. Surely it is a nonsense that in any given congregation the visiting preachers are nearly always drawn from the same denomination and tradition. Surely it is ridiculous that most ministers restrict their reading to authors and publishing houses with whom they expect to agree. Surely it must be sinful that the vast majority of believers never share communion with their neighbouring brothers and sisters from other congregations. Surely it is pathetic that the probability of most Protestants visiting a Catholic church is only equalled by the chance of them entering a brothel.

In some localities inter-denominational Bible study groups exist during Lent. These could usefully be developed so that all the believers in any street or village regularly meet to pray, study, and eat together. These groups could either replace congregational house groups for more of the year, or they could alternate throughout the year. This means working at relationships within our own congregation, and simultaneously building contacts with the wider body in our own immediate locality. The inner twelve managed it, we could at least try. We need to understand the phrase 'the local church' to mean all the believers in a locality and not any one congregation; and I think believers should have this double commitment—to their own congregation and to an unorganised expression of the local church in their street, suburb, small town, or village. (I do not mean by this an existing society or parachurch group which represents a particular sector or emphasis of the church.)

I am convinced that we should be praying and working towards a community in every locality which will reflect both the variety and the oneness of God through all the different denominational congregations which make it up, so that the church is seen to be one, but more than one. All I mean by this is that all the believers in a locality should know each other; should meet regularly to eat, pray, worship, socialise, and help each other practically; should occasionally worship locally in a tradition and congregation other than their own; and should covenant as congregations never to duplicate activities or do apart what it is legitimate to do together.

I plead with all Christian leaders to begin experimenting with an unstructured community where the different congregations scrap their individual main Sunday service several times a year and instead meet together to celebrate the great Christian festivals, to share the eucharist, and to recognise, confirm and maintain their innate oneness.

I beg that all ministers slowly nurture an unstructured community within which all the different congregations show their appreciation of all the other parts of the one body by praying for them in every service, by regularly sharing each others' pulpits, by ensuring that there is no public criticism, and by frequently and regularly meeting in mixed small groups.

I pray for the day when in every town and area there is an unstructured community whose members and leaders agree to disagree about many things, but agree that they are all one only in Christ Jesus.

If unity is our priority we will maintain such a community, where all the different local leaders demonstrate this priority by sacrificing time in their own small kingdoms to set the example of eating together, praying together and sharing hospitality. A community whose members know all the other members living nearby, and who follow their leaders' example in eating, praying and sharing together. A community filled with people whose aim is to build up the one body rather than their own little part. A community characterised by love, not slander; by congregational self-effacement, not ambition; by gracious tolerance, not theological bigotry; by mutual hospitality, not mutual suspicion; by common appreciation, not critical arrogance; and by a constant sense of wonder at Christ's death which made us all eternally one, rather than perpetual amazement at the possibility that any of 'them' might be welcomed into heaven.

What would the man or woman in the street make of such a community? We cannot say with certainty that he will be challenged, but as our present divisions only serve to underline his disbelief, evangelistic concern alone should make us keen to see for ourselves how John 17:23 works out in practice.

What would the Man in heaven think of such a community? Would he prefer it to our schism, our ambition and our pharisaical love for doctrinal nit-picking? Would he be pleased? Would he bless our desire for unity more than he blesses our present individualism and division? Would he think such an unorganised group was the full answer to his John 17:23 prayer? I'd like to find out.

And what would the men and women in the pews and pulpits of our land think of such visible oneness? Those who have tried it declare it to be both good and delightful. But I know many ministers who fight it tooth and nail. However, as Christ died to make us one, I believe we have a duty to disagree lovingly with those leaders who would rather be a shark in a garden pond than a tadpole in God's almighty ocean. And I believe that we have an over-riding responsibility to kneel shoulder to shoulder with all God's people, refusing to have any fewer brothers and sisters than God has sons and daughters.